Illustrations by Brian Dumm
Design by Melody Taylor | GraphicSolutions, Inc.

ISBN: 978-1-59850-192-6 | Library of Congress Number: 2015956428
10 9 8
Printed in the United States

HI! I'M HUNTER.

HAS ANYONE EVER TOLD YOU TO "USE YOUR HEAD?"

I wasn't really sure what that meant, but somehow I felt bad about myself when I heard it.

I used to think something was wrong with the way my brain works, but then I discovered a tool that has helped me to feel a lot better about myself.

This is the story about how I learned to appreciate my special brain... a story about how I figured out what it means to

"USE MY HEAD."

MY BRAIN

Everyone's brain is amazing and works in different ways. I'm often told that I'm creative because I have so many great ideas.

I've also been told many times to **PAY ATTENTION,** but actually...

....I'm very aware of what's going on around me. I seem to notice everything because I don't want to miss something important.

My brain is so full of information that I always have something interesting to think about.

MY MIND IS LIKE A T.V. WITH LOTS OF CHANNELS.

I know that having a brain like mine is really special, but it can also be frustrating. Sometimes when I'm at school trying to listen to my teacher, my mind switches to a different channel.

Then I make mistakes later because I missed important information while I was on the wrong channel. Now I know that this is what my teacher means when she tells me to **"PAY ATTENTION."**

It seems like my special **BRAIN WORKS REALLY FAST.**

I have lots of energy and enthusiasm, but that makes it harder for me to stop and think before I do things. One day when I was excited, I threw a pillow in the air and broke a lamp.

And sometimes when I'm supposed to be still, I feel like I have so much energy inside my body that **I MIGHT EXPLODE** if I don't get to move around soon!

My family, friends, and teachers are sometimes frustrated with my energy and enthusiasm.

The truth is, I used to feel like there was something wrong with me because I didn't realize that these CHALLENGES were part of what makes me so CREATIVE, ENERGETIC, and ENTHUSIASTIC. Now I feel better about myself because one day I had the best idea I've ever had!

THE GREAT IDEA!

It was Saturday and I was watching my favorite T.V. show when my little brother, Josh, picked up the remote control and started changing channels.

As I took the remote control from Josh and used it to return to my program, the idea came like a flash of lightning.

I NEED A REMOTE CONTROL
FOR MY BRAIN!

CHANNEL CHANGER

I took a block of wood and some markers to make a "channel changer," just like the one for the T.V.

When I noticed that my thoughts were focused on the wrong thing. I used my remote control to change back to the right channel.

In math class when I started thinking about what I was going to eat for lunch, I pushed the channel changer button and switched my brain back to the math channel.

MORE BUTTONS

My next idea came on a rainy afternoon when I was watching a movie. Again, Josh grabbed the T.V. remote control, and this time he pushed "pause" and then the "fast forward" button.

Suddenly, I realized that there was so MUCH MORE I could do with the remote control that I made for my brain. I began to think of buttons that I could add.

PAUSE

My first addition to the remote control was "pause." I learned to push this button before I did or said something that could get me into trouble. I used "pause" before I threw something in the house, before I spoke out-of-turn in class, and before I ran out into the street after my soccer ball.

The "pause" button gave me a chance to think before I did something. At first, it was really hard to remember, but the more I practiced, the easier it was.

FAST FORWARD

I also thought about how using "fast forward" on the remote control shows me what happens later in a movie. I decided to put a button on my brain remote control to help me see what might happen in the future.

I used both of the new buttons the next day when my football was on the top shelf of the bookcase. I was just about to climb up to get the ball when I remembered to push "pause" then "fast forward." I realized that the bookshelf could fall over on me so I decided to ask for help.

THE SHOULDS

But even with lots of practice, I don't always remember to push the "pause" and "fast forward" buttons before I do or say something, and **DISASTER!**

Of course I know that everyone makes mistakes, but sometimes when I mess up... I end up with something I call the SHOULDS.

I think...

"I should have said something else."

"I should have done something different."

"I should not have done that."

"I should be more careful."

The SHOULDS always make me feel **DISCOURAGED!**

I had a bad case of the SHOULDS after a field trip to the zoo. It was a special occasion so I was allowed to take a can of Fizzola Cola for lunch.

While I was waiting in line for lunch, I threw my lunch in the air three times, but only caught it once. When I finally opened the can of Fizzola Cola, it sprayed everywhere!

At home later, Mom saw the cola on my shirt and the SHOULDS all over my face. She said..."Hunter, I think people are kind of like drinks. Some people are serious like tea. Other people are like fruit punch – sweet and cheerful all the time. Then there are the Fizzola Cola people, excited and fun, but when they get shaken up, they have to work harder to calm down.

I DECIDED TO ADD A BUTTON TO HELP ME WITH THE SHOULDS AND ONE FOR CALMING DOWN.

REWIND

I thought of using a rewind button to go back and remember what I was doing and thinking before I messed up and think about what I could have done differently. Then I can make a plan for how to make a better choice next time.

Mom really liked this idea and now sometimes she lets me use **"REWIND"** to say or do something over – before I get in trouble. It's like getting a second chance and it sure helps with the SHOULDS.

SLOW MOTION

I decided to add a "slow motion" button to remind me to move slower and be more relaxed.

I learned that if I took a slow deep breath and counted to 10 when I pushed the button, it worked even better.

I practiced using **"SLOW MOTION"** at my birthday party when I was opening presents. I was really glad I slowed down because it gave me a chance to thank everyone, and it made the fun last a lot longer.

COACH

The inspiration for the next button on my brain remote control came from my baseball coach.

Once I struck out three times, dropped the ball over and over, and tripped over second base... all in one game!

I wanted to give up and quit the team.
Until...

Coach Cooper told me, “All athletes have bad days now and then – especially when they are young and still learning. Keep trying and learn from your mistakes.”

I added a **"COACH"** button and learned to push it when I need encouragement to try harder, when I need to remember that it's OK to make mistakes, and when I need to come up with a plan for doing better. It turns out that coaching is not just helpful for sports, but on the playground, in class, and at home.

ZAP!

Our school counselor told my class that negative thoughts have the power to make you feel discouraged. I realized that I often had thoughts like...

"There's something wrong with me."
"People don't like me."
"I'm a bad kid,"
or "I'll never get it right."

These thoughts are almost always wrong, but if we are not careful, we can start believing them.

I put a button on my brain remote control called "ZAP!" so I could get rid of those negative thoughts before I had a chance to believe them.

WAY TO GO

The last button was actually my mom's idea. She said, "Hunter, you don't have to wait for other people like Coach Cooper or me to tell you when you've done something right. Why don't you add a button that will remind you to notice when you are successful?"

I named it "Way to Go!" and I ended up using it a lot more than I thought I would.

SCHOOL BUS
SCHOOL BUS

IN CONTROL

With practice, I have become so good at using my brain remote control that I don't even need to have it with me. It's kind of like I have an invisible one with me all the time.

I know that I am the only one who has the power to use my remote control. No one else can make me think, feel, or do something. I choose which buttons to use.

So that's my story about how my brain remote control changed my life.

THE MORE I USE IT, THE BETTER I GET ALONG WITH MY FRIENDS, PARENTS, AND TEACHERS.

I don't get into trouble as much and I'm doing better in school. I still make mistakes and I'm still frustrated when I forget to use the remote control buttons.

BUT MY AMAZING REMOTE CONTROL
HAS HELPED ME TO REALIZE THAT

I AM AN AMAZING PERSON

AND SO ARE YOU!

ALSO AVAILABLE FROM YOUTHLIGHT

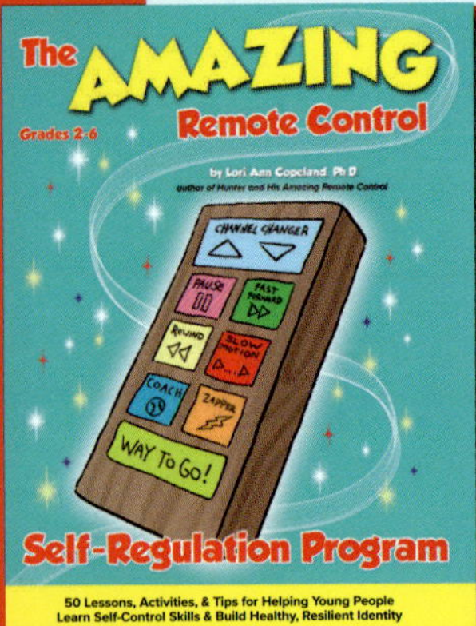

The Amazing Remote Control (Leader's Guide)

50 lessons, activities & tips for helping young people learn self-control skills and build healthy, resilient identities.

Item Code: HUNTLG ISBN: 978-1-59850-193-3

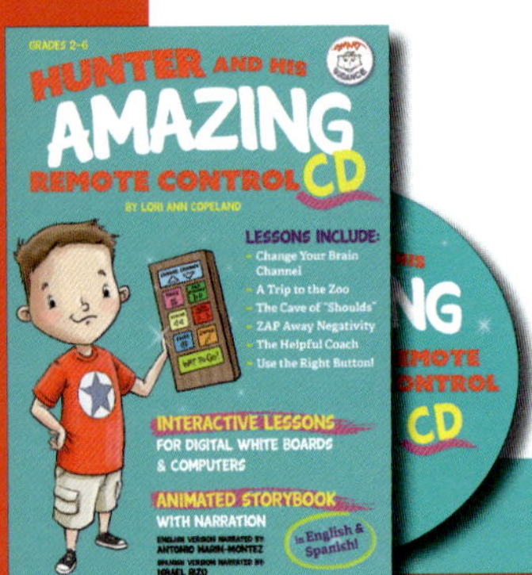

Hunter and His Amazing Remote Control Interactive Lessons

Available on CD or Online Access

Animated storybook in both English and Spanish PLUS 6 interactive lessons to teach and review self-control skills.

Item Code (CD): HUNTCD (Online Access): HUNTOA

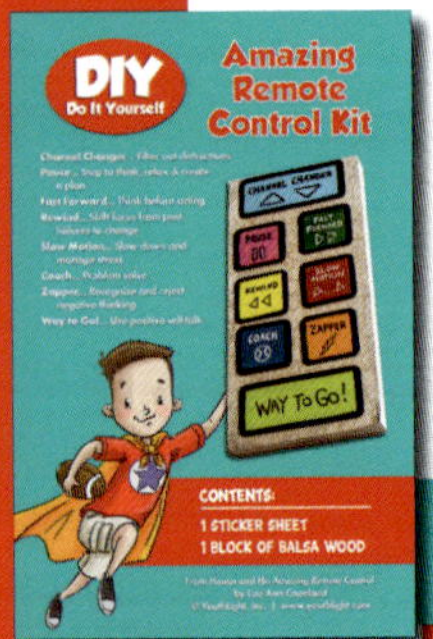

Amazing Remote Control Kit

Includes a full-color sticker sheet of all of the remote control buttons introduced in this storybook along with a block of balsa wood to adhere the stickers as each self-control skill is taught.

Item Code: REMOTE

Amazing Remote Control Wall Display

Includes all 8 remote control buttons with strategy reminders printed on cardstock and cut to size. Creates a 3 foot wall display.

Item Code: HUNTWD

P.O. Box 115 Chapin, SC 29036
www.youthlight.com